LEAN SIX SIGMA

IN 60 MINUTES

For Nurses & Leaders

Fast & effective tools for beginners, leaders, & executives
read in 60 minutes & apply methods on same day

Arizona Institute of Management
Raaaj T Chaugule

Lean Six Sigma in 60 minutes for Nurses & Leaders

November 2024 Edition
Library of Congress Control Number: 9798987702178
Electronic eBook version ISBN: 979-8-9877021-3-0
Paperback Book version ISBN: 979-8-9877021-7-8
Hardcover Book version ISBN: 979-8-9877021-5-4

Books or eBooks are available for press reviews, author reviews, special prices for bulk quantities, for classrooms or education, government training programs, corporate training programs, please contact, Arizona Institute of Management, City of Chandler, State of Arizona, USA, www.AZinstitute.net

Dedicated to all the amazing nurses that work so tirelessly to heal & care not only the patients but the families & friends as well. Lilian & Yoviannah who continue to encourage me to share my light with the world. And to my readers!

Acknowledgements

It takes a lot of expertise & experience to make a book like this a reality. Thanks to our editing team, graphics artists, the proofing team & everyone at Arizona Institute of Management.

Thanks to the United States Copyright Office & the Library of Congress. Thanks to images by Anastasia Gepp from Pixabay, Instagram - nastya_gepp. Also thanks to the distributors who bring share this light with readers.

About the publisher & author

Arizona Institute of Management, provides training, coaching & advisory services to for-profit, non-profit & government organizations to improve today & tomorrow for current & future generations on our beautiful planet.

Raaaj T. Chaugule is an American professional with over two decades of hands-on experience at Fortune 100 companies in USA, such as Ford Motor Company, Ford Motor Credit Company, Providence Health, State of California, Education Management Corporation, Banner Health.

While he is honored by distinguished awards, from Ford's Customer Driven Quality Award to Banner's Amazement Award, he is respected by his peers & clients as a Problem-solver, Innovator, Transformer, Disrupter, Thought-leader in Healthcare, Education, Call Center, Finance, Automotive, & Energy industries.

Raaaj's strengths as a big-picture thinker is deeply-rooted in his multi-industry & global experience in Quality, Safety, Product Development, Automation, Operations, Process Engineering, Enterprise Project & Program Management, Customer Service Level Management, Lean Six Sigma making him a trusted partner, leader & an executive coach for individuals, leaders, & organizations.

He is very passionate to share & inspire individuals & organizations to improve, transform, innovate, succeed & be happy.

How to best use this book

Read & Apply learnings Today!

This book focuses on basic understandings & practical applications of Lean & Six Sigma for leaders & problem-solvers.

Read

✓ At first, just read through all the pages & grasp the concepts.

✓ Its okay, if you do not remember everything. Idea is to raise your awareness.

✓ You may have a few light bulb moments. That's good! Jot them down before you forget them!

Apply

✓ Step 1: Pick a simple problem or situation for practice.

✓ Step 2: Go to the Lean Six Sigma chapter, follow each phase step-by-step & apply it to your problem or situation.

Power of Clarity

Have you noticed in the last few decades, there are certain individuals or organizations, despite competition, stand apart from their peers. All of them have the same platform, resources, market, technology & resources available to them. Yet a handful surpass their peers to deliver exceptional results. What is their super power?

This power is clarity

Clarity, on its own is simple, but to obtain it, in the midst of chaos, ideas, and complexities around us, is priceless. Without it, many spend unsurmountable time, effort & resources to deliver less than desirable results & sometimes more chaos. Billions of dollars are spent to pursue & seek clarity that provides guidance to align your strengths and resources primarily to survive, but few take it to the next level – to thrive.

In this book, you will find invaluable nuggets, when applied appropriately, will increase your chances to thrive & shine.

Table of Contents

The insights gained from this book on Lean Six Sigma are equivalent to a Yellow Belt level of expertise.

♥

Visit AIM's website for details on Certification

Chapter 1 Introduction

A nurse, A pioneer, A legend

Florence Nightingale

A nurse, a statistician and the founder of modern nursing.

During the Crimean War, Florence Nightingale transformed an overcrowded military hospital by enforcing strict hygiene practices like handwashing, cleaning wounds, and removing waste. Her efforts reduced death rate from 42% to 2%, proving lifesaving importance of sanitation & ventilation.

Her key contributions:

- **Revolutionized Nursing:** Established modern nursing practices, emphasizing hygiene and patient care.
- **Improved Sanitation:** Drastically reduced death rates by promoting cleanliness in hospitals during the Crimean War.
- **Founded Nursing Education:** Opened the Nightingale School of Nursing in 1860, setting professional standards.
- **Pioneered Statistical Analysis:** Used data visualization, like pie charts, polar area diagrams, to advocate for healthcare reforms.
- **Advocated Public Health:** Influenced global healthcare policies on sanitation and preventive care.

Nurses have transformed healthcare & will continue to do so.

Meet

**Nurse
Amy**

**Charge Nurse
Claudia**

**Nurse Director
Linda**

Amy

Amy is one of those people who got into nursing to make a real difference in patient's lives, but recently, it's been tough. She's spending more time dealing with inefficient processes and "just the way things are done" than actually caring for her patients.

Then one day, Amy's hospital introduces Lean Six Sigma. At first, she's skeptical. It sounds like another management buzzword, right? But her manager, Claudia, tells her it's all about making her life easier and giving her more time with her patients, which gets Amy interested and learns about a Six Sigma tool called DMAIC, short for Define, Measure, Analyze, Improve, and Control.

Easier life in 5 steps, she exclaims, "I am curious now." In her mind, she says to herself, "Wonder if I can apply this to my personal life as well?"

Yes! You can apply this method to your professional & any aspect of your personal life, finances, career, relationships, and more.

Linda

Amy takes a break to grab her afternoon treat. While walking to the coffee shop, Amy recalls her best friend, Linda, mentioning about training & certification in process improvement. What was it, she wondered, as she picks up her afternoon Pumpkin Spice Latte. Was it ... Yellow, Green, Pink Belt? She sits down at a table, next to the glass window, overlooking the fountain, and texts her friend as she sips her delightful latte.

Amy: Hey Linda, how are you ... long time

Linda: Doing great, perfect timing. How are you?

Amy: Great. Perfect timing for what...?

Linda: Just got promoted

Amy: Congratulations!

Linda: Super excited. Thank you, thank you... so what's on your mind?

Amy: Remember you got some belt certificate in process improvement

Linda: Yes. That is the reason for my promotion

Amy: Wait what... how... why... huh ?!!!

Linda: Received my Yellow Belt in Lean Six Sigma, applied the 5-step method for improving our safety & patient satisfaction scores, got recognized a few months ago by our CNO, and now this!!!

Amy: Wow! So happy for you. Want more details, call you later.

The power duo ... 1

During her lunch break, Amy ponders, "I am constantly encouraged to pursue critical-thinking to deliver the best care and I often use the SBAR when starting care, transferring care, writing reports, etc."

Do I really need DMAIC?

SBAR - Situation, Background, Assessment, Recommendation
DMAIC - Define, Measure, Analyze, Improve, Control

Both SBAR & DMAIC are powerful tools, but they serve different purposes.

SBAR is a Communication Tool	**DMAIC** is a Problem-solving or Improvement Tool

The power duo ... 2

When to Use?

SBAR – In time-sensitive or emergency situations, this is a better choice, as it's designed for quick, effective communication. It's ideal when starting patient care, patient handovers, escalating a patient's condition, writing reports, communicating with other providers.

DMAIC – Use when improving safety, quality, or efficiency, such as reducing medication errors, wait times, or streamlining discharge processes. It's ideal for tackling persistent or complex issues that require a systematic approach and uses critical thinking.

SBAR Strengths:

Clarity and Precision – SBAR ensures that the message is clear, structured, and actionable.

Efficiency – helpful in high-stress situations, SBAR reduces misunderstandings, leading to faster and more effective responses.

DMAIC Strengths:

Systematic Problem Solving – DMAIC encourages a deep dive into the root causes of problems, leading to sustainable, long-term improvements.

Data-Driven Decisions – The methodology relies on data to guide decisions, reducing errors and waste.

Amy & Claudia ... 1

Amy takes a fun & exciting training. The next day, at the huddle, their Charge Nurse, Claudia, amongst other things mentions about a recurring issue: medication delays. Patients were supposed to get their meds within 30 minutes, but delays were common, leading to frustration & even errors.

Amy, speaks up & says, "Hey Claudia, could we use the 5-step DMAIC for this?" Claudia's face lights up, and says, "Oh if you can stop these delays, I am buying lunch". The momentum builds, Amy forms a small team of 3 colleagues, they meet up later to tackle Medication Delays.

Amy sees how ...

The **Define** phase lets everyone sit down together to clarify the issue without pointing fingers.

In the **Measure** phase, they track just how often meds are delayed and why. Turns out, supplies were often not stocked correctly, or orders took too long to process.

Amy & Claudia ... 2

Then comes the **Analyze** phase, where Amy and her team dig deeper to conduct root-cause analysis. They find that one of the main reasons is a complicated inventory process. Every shift, they're double-checking supplies because they never know what will be missing.

The **Improve** phase is Amy's favorite. Instead of endless paperwork or another meeting, they actually change things. They streamline the inventory process, add reminders to restock supplies at specific times, and automate medication requests.

Finally, the **Control** phase helps keep the changes in place. They monitor the new system to make sure it's working as planned. Amy notices that, with fewer delays, her stress level goes down. She's able to check on her patients more regularly, and her patients seem happier too.

Over the next few months, Amy and her team see a huge difference. She's spending less time on avoidable problems and more on actual patient care. Medication delays go down, patient satisfaction goes up, and she doesn't go home every night feeling completely drained. **Yay nursing !**

Amy & Liliana

Patient satisfaction trends rise, and is noticed by her hospital CNO Liliana. Amy & her team gets recognized by CNO & other Hospital leaders.

A few days later, as Amy heads for her Café Latte, she realizes that Lean Six Sigma isn't just some management concept; it's like a secret weapon that helps her and her team do what they love — caring for patients.

For Amy, nursing is less about putting out fires and more about supporting people—why she became a nurse in the first place.

Amy now realizes that Lean Six Sigma is more than just a method; it's a path to becoming the nurse she's always aspired to be.

Versatile

Lean Six Sigma is one of the most powerful management tools in manufacturing & service industries.

any size

any organization

any sector

You can apply these methods almost anywhere:

- To improve Quality, Safety, Customer Experience & Loyalty
- For-profits can improve Top line, bottom line or both
- Non-profits & Governments can stretch the dollar to do more with limited funds

Lean Six Sigma is versatile & at the core of several improvements, transformations, & innovation programs in any industry.

Lean Six Sigma Genesis

- Walter Shewhart a physicist, engineer and statistician, the father of statistical process control, introduced it in early 20th century at **Bell**.
- Bill Smith, is often referred as the "Father of Six Sigma", in 1980's, he suggested to improve quality by reducing process variation to Motorola's CEO, Bob Galvin, for products, processes, services and administration. As a result, **Motorola** saved several billion dollars.
- In the 1990s, **Allied Signal**'s CEO, Larry Bossidy, adopted Six Sigma.
- Shortly, **GE**'s CEO, Jack Welch, adopted this innovative system.
- Lean Manufacturing and processes were introduced by Henry **Ford** in early 1900s later adopted by Japanese industries and further developed by **Deming, Ohno, & others.**

Today Lean Six Sigma is successfully used in automotive, aerospace, aircraft, biotech, chemical, clothes, shoes, electronics, construction equipment, foods, metals, paper, textile, wood product companies for quality, management & improvement.

To name a few: Amazon, Samsung, McKesson, Abbott, 3M, Chevron, Department of Defense, Ford, Bank of America, Red Cross.

Chapter 2 Overview

What is Lean Six Sigma?

Lean Six Sigma combines Lean & Six Sigma methods for improving a service or product by minimizing waste & variation.

Lean

Minimizes Waste

Six Sigma

Minimizes Variation

Lean Six Sigma Principles

While Lean focuses on spotting & eliminating wasteful activities, Six Sigma enables us to reduce variation by identifying & addressing the root-causes.

Some key understandings & notable principles in Lean Six Sigma:

Voice of Customer - focus on customer & understand expectations

Customer Journey – view processes from a customer's point of view

Non-value-added elements - spot & eliminate them

Data-driven - analyze, solve & manage improvements using data

Team-driven - build & engage small teams & enable them to succeed

Pursue Continuous Improvement – be current, never stop improving

Lean Six Sigma Competencies & Roles

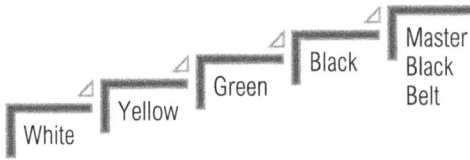

LSS as a competency, has several certification levels known as Belts:

White Belt
- Has basic understandings of Lean Six Sigma concept & terminologies to pursue improvements in their job function

Yellow Belt
- Skilled in Basic Lean Six Sigma
- Leads smaller projects within a single functional area of a department or supports Green or Black Belt projects

Green Belt
- Skilled in Lean Six Sigma, Basic Analytics, Facilitation, & inter-personal skills
- Leads single department projects, supports Black Belt projects

Black Belt
- Skilled in Lean Six Sigma, Advanced Analytics, Project Management, Facilitation, & inter-personal skills
- Leads projects across multiple departments. Trains up to Green Belts & coaches LSS project teams

Master Black Belt
- Trains & coaches all Belts, Champions, Executives. Leads LSS Program & multiple Black Belt projects
- Works with Business & Operations Leaders, Managers & Executives, in strategic & tactical planning

Lean Six Sigma Other Roles

Executive Leaders: White Belt trained, commits resources, removes barriers & challenges, to support LSS projects

Champion: White Belt trained, plans & oversees LSS Program deployment and Projects across the organization

Stakeholders: Individuals whose interests may be positively or negatively affected as a result of the project

Subject Matter Experts (SMEs): Are engaged to consult or are part of the LSS project team. Experts internal or external that can help in deeper level understandings, solutions, etc.

Chapter 3 Lean

Lean

As mentioned, Lean methodology focuses on spotting & eliminating wasteful activities. It is customer-centered and helps you to take an objective look at your organization, service, product or process.

Amongst many, there a few that are popular, widely-used and highly effective Lean Tools, namely:

- SIPOC
- Types of Waste
- Value Stream Analysis
- 5S

Note: Lean tools can be used independently.

Lean – SIPOC tool

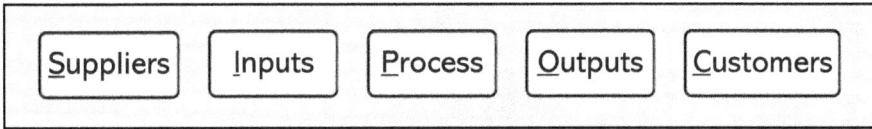

| Suppliers | Inputs | Process | Outputs | Customers |

One of the most important management tools, provides clarity & helps to align everyone. SIPOC is a very insightful visual tool that helps you to create a Big Picture of your product or service.

SIPOC is an acronym and consists of 5 key elements:

- **Supplier** – Who provides all the inputs required for your Process
- **Inputs** – What are the inputs required for your Process
- **Process** – Is a sequence of steps required to create an Output or a desired product or service
- **Output** – A product or service that is provided to your Customer
- **Customer** – A person or organization, internal or external, that consumes or utilizes products or services

Tip: To keep it simple, pick 1 service or product as an output to create a SIPOC. Ex: Milk shake at a fast food

SIPOC – Illustration

SIPOC for Serving Coffee

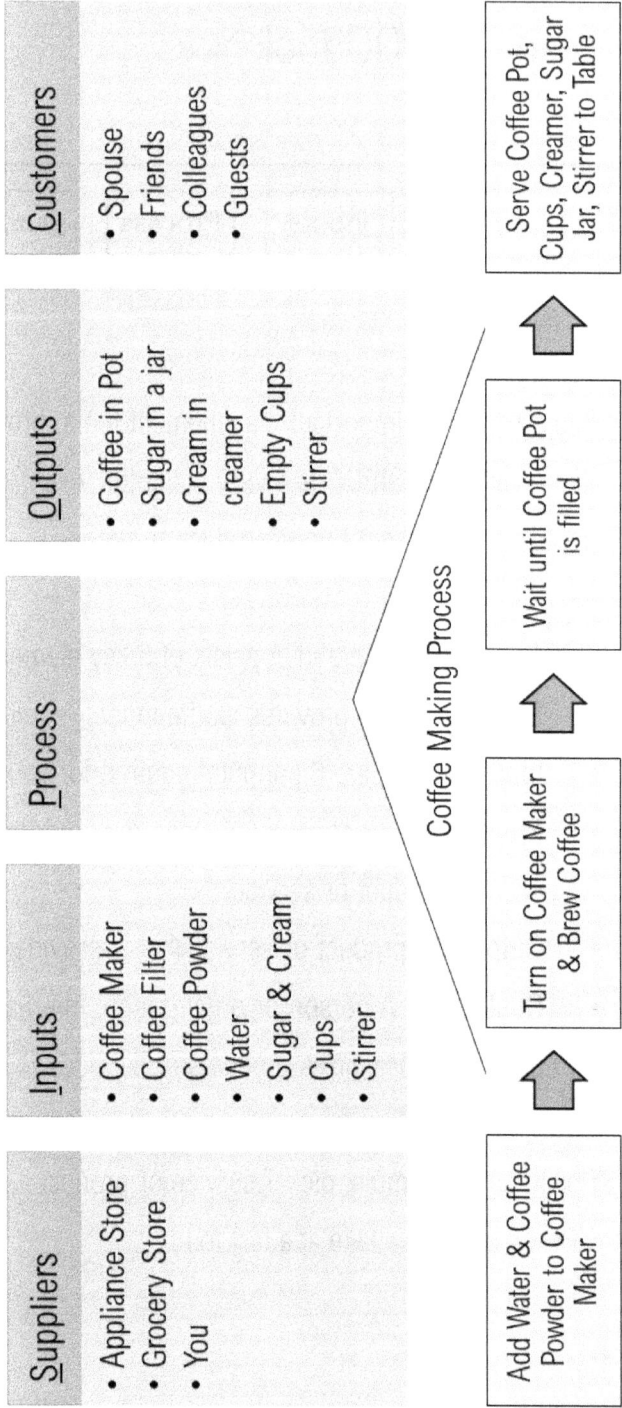

Suppliers	Inputs	Process	Outputs	Customers
• Appliance Store	• Coffee Maker		• Coffee in Pot	• Spouse
• Grocery Store	• Coffee Filter		• Sugar in a jar	• Friends
• You	• Coffee Powder		• Cream in creamer	• Colleagues
	• Water		• Empty Cups	• Guests
	• Sugar & Cream		• Stirrer	
	• Cups			
	• Stirrer			

Coffee Making Process

Add Water & Coffee Powder to Coffee Maker	⇨	Turn on Coffee Maker & Brew Coffee	⇨	Wait until Coffee Pot is filled	⇨	Serve Coffee Pot, Cups, Creamer, Sugar Jar, Stirrer to Table

What is Process?

A sequence of steps taken to provide a Service or Product. Processes are written or visualized. Basic Process includes:

- People – Skills, Experience, Talent,…

- Machines – Equipment, Trucks, Systems, Tools, ..

- Materials – Facilities, Stationery, Forms, Fuel, ..

- Methods – Procedures, Policies, Safety, Recipes, ..

Note:
- You can write a process or create a process diagram on paper or in Word, Excel, Visio or PowerPoint software.
- Budget, Safety & Quality is in every element of a process & is defined by the organization.

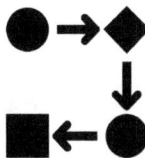

Process – Illustration

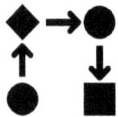

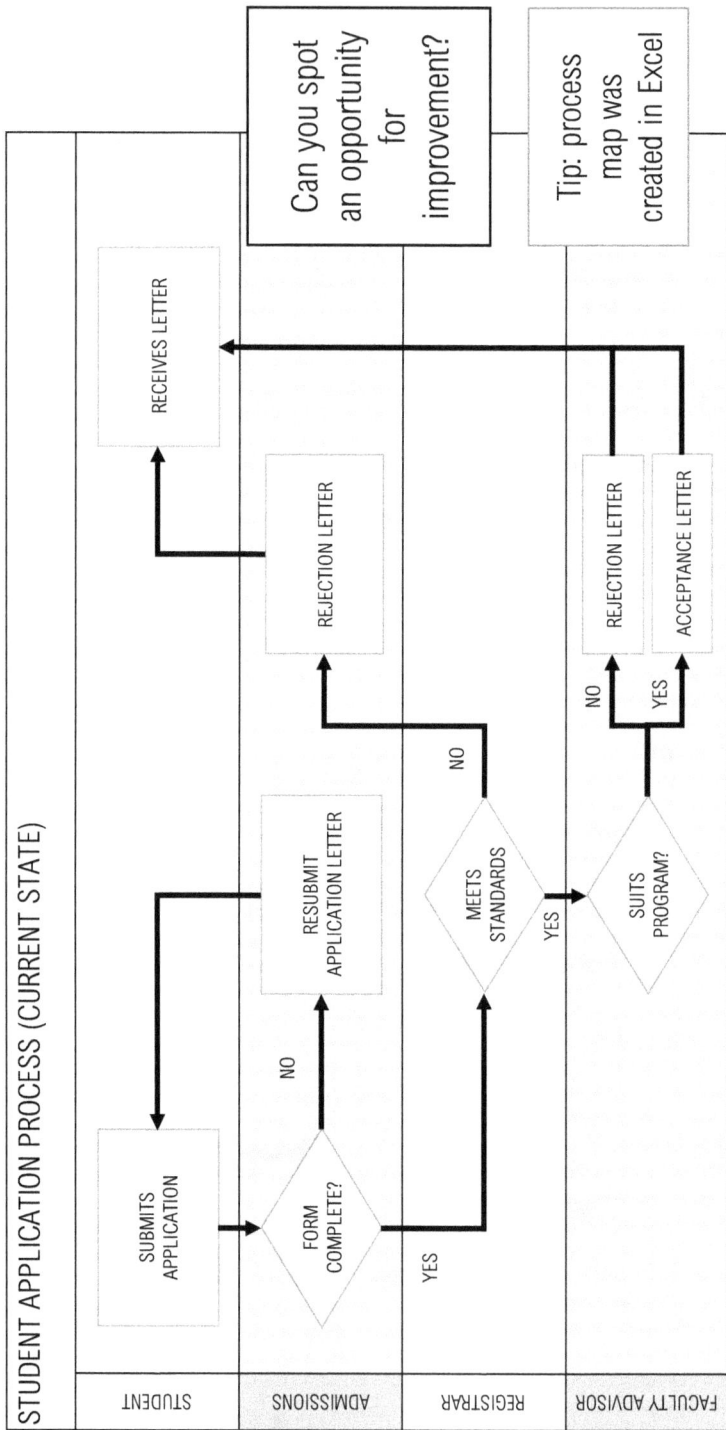

STUDENT APPLICATION PROCESS (CURRENT STATE)

Can you spot an opportunity for improvement?

Tip: process map was created in Excel

Lane	Steps
STUDENT	SUBMITS APPLICATION → RECEIVES LETTER
ADMISSIONS	FORM COMPLETE? → (NO) RESUBMIT APPLICATION LETTER / (YES) → REJECTION LETTER
REGISTRAR	MEETS STANDARDS → (NO) → (YES)
FACULTY ADVISOR	SUITS PROGRAM? → (NO) REJECTION LETTER / (YES) ACCEPTANCE LETTER

Process – Illustration

Business Continuity Planning Process Diagram

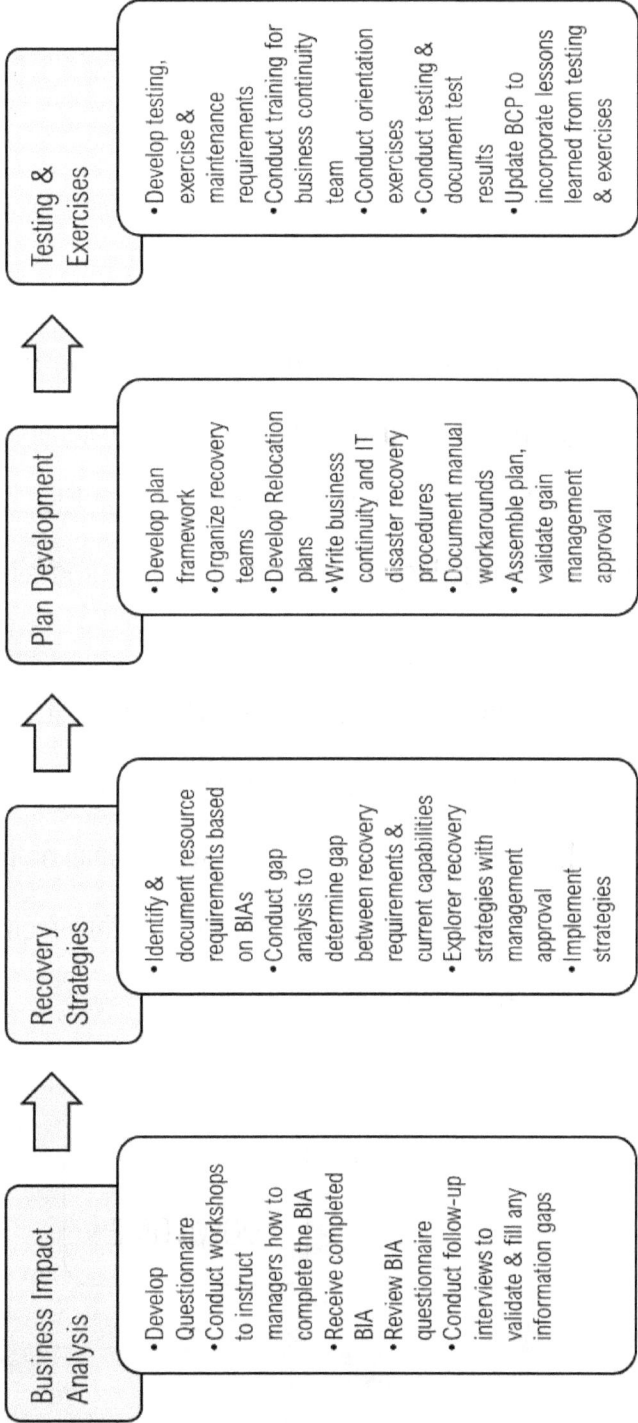

Business Impact Analysis
- Develop Questionnaire
- Conduct workshops to instruct managers how to complete the BIA
- Receive completed BIA
- Review BIA questionnaire
- Conduct follow-up interviews to validate & fill any information gaps

Recovery Strategies
- Identify & document resource requirements based on BIAs
- Conduct gap analysis to determine gap between recovery requirements & current capabilities
- Explorer recovery strategies with management approval
- Implement strategies

Plan Development
- Develop plan framework
- Organize recovery teams
- Develop Relocation plans
- Write business continuity and IT disaster recovery procedures
- Document manual workarounds
- Assemble plan, validate gain management approval

Testing & Exercises
- Develop testing, exercise & maintenance requirements
- Conduct training for business continuity team
- Conduct orientation exercises
- Conduct testing & document test results
- Update BCP to incorporate lessons learned from testing & exercises

Lean – Types of Waste

Detect the following types of wastes, to reduce Non-Value-Add elements.

- **Defects** - Mistakes or errors leading to reworking

- **Over-production** - Creating too much material, information

- **Waiting** - Waiting on information or materials

- **Non-utilization** - Not recognizing talent or ideas from all organization levels

- **Transportation** - Moving Material or Information too much or too far

- **Inventory** - Too much material or information to provide service

- **Motion** - Moving people to access material or information

- **Excess processing** - Processing more than required to achieve desired output

acronym is
DOWNTIME

Lean Types of Waste – Illustration

Wastes	Description	Office Examples
Defects	Mistakes or errors leading to reworking	Order entry errors, change orders, invoice errors
Over-production	Creating too much material, information	Printing more than needed
Waiting	Waiting on information or materials	System downtime, slow system response, approvals
Non-utilization	Not recognizing talent or ideas from all organization levels	Limited employee empowerment for basic tasks, inadequate business tools
Transportation	Moving Material or Information too much or too far	Excessive email attachments, multiple hand-offs, multiple approvals
Inventory	Too much material or information to provide service	Too much Supplies, Forms, Printed materials, Subscriptions
Motion	Moving people to access material or information	Walking to printer, fax, other offices, central paper filing
Excess processing	Processing more than required to achieve desired output	Too many reports, Color copies, duplicate copies, expediting, packaging, mailings

Lean – Value Stream Analysis

No one wants to pay more than they need. Value is doing things in the most effective, economical & efficient way.

Types:

- **Value-Add (VA)** – Elements necessary to meet customer expectations. Example: Adding cheese in a cheese burger
- **Business Value-Add (BVA)** – Elements necessary to provide the product or service Example: Cash Register
- **Non-Value-Add (NVA)** – Customer may not value or prefer to pay for these services. Example: cost of serving food in fancy dishes at a fast food restaurant.

In a process, evaluate every step & its elements, and determine if they are VA, BVA or NVA. Non-Value-Add should ideally be less than 5%. Reducing NVA, improves customer satisfaction, competitiveness & increases customer demand.

Non-Value
Add

Value
Add

Lean – 5S

5S method is very simple & effective for identifying & eliminating waste, and increasing efficiency in any workplace.

Steps include:

- **Sort** - Eliminate what is not needed

- **Straighten** - Organize what remains

- **Shine** - Clean work area and keep it clean

- **Standardize** - Establish consistency across similar work areas

- **Sustain** - Maintain, Audit, Continually Improve

Note: Workspace can be either physical, virtual or digital

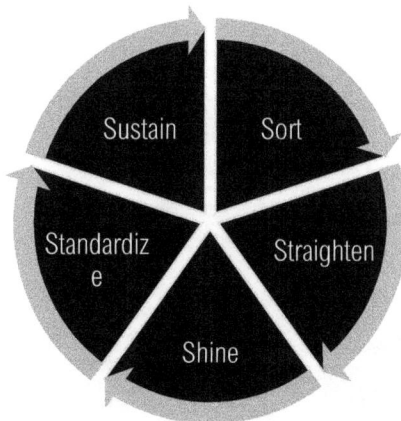

Chapter 4 Six Sigma

Six Sigma

Six Sigma philosophy helps us focus on what is critical to customer, use data-driven tools, pursue root-cause, find solution, & prevent it from recurring.

Six Sigma methodologies

- DMAIC for problem-solving for existing products or services
- DMADV for new products or services

We will focus on DMAIC in this book.

Six Sigma DMAIC

DMAIC is framework used for problem-solving. Has 5 sequential phases to deliver results.

1. **Define** – Define the problem
2. **Measure** – Collect the data
3. **Analyze** – Analyze the data, conduct Root-cause analysis
4. **Improve** – Identify a solution, verify it, implement
5. **Control** – Monitor performance, Sustain the solution

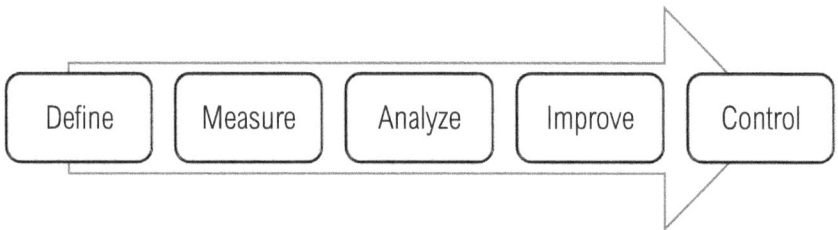

| Define | Measure | Analyze | Improve | Control |

Popular Six Sigma terminologies

Mean or Average

- Is the average data value of the population

- An average value closer to the target value is better

Sigma or Standard Deviation (Represented as σ)

- The Standard Deviation, a measure of how spread out are the numbers from the mean

- Smaller the better, means less variation in your results

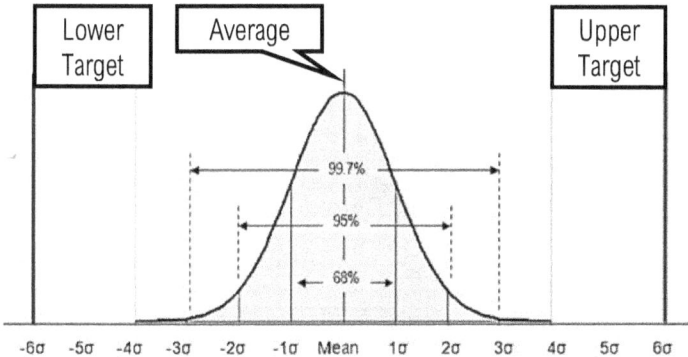

Histogram Chart is used for visualizing or plotting
data collected for a specific measure

Mean & Sigma are calculated & shown to understand variation.

Upper & Lower target values are also shown
to understand if values are within the target range.

Popular Six Sigma terminologies

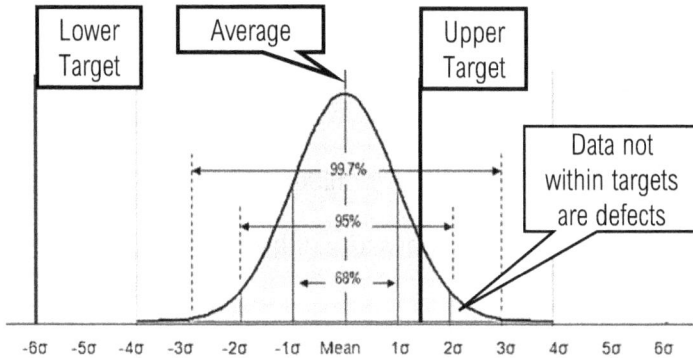

DPMO

- Number of Defects Per Million Opportunities

- $DPMO = \dfrac{\text{Number of Defects}}{\text{Number of Defect Opportunities}} \times 1{,}000{,}000$

Six Sigma in perspective

At Six Sigma level, there are 3.4 Defects Per Million

Service Level performance

Process Target is 2 minutes or less. 900 out of 1000 transactions met target. Yield is 90%, DPMO is 100,000, Sigma Level is 2.78

Airline Bags Delivery performance

In 2015 for 3.5+ Billion passengers, Yield was 99.35% bags delivered. Sounds like a very good performance, right? Let's see, this indicates total bags lost were 22+ Million. Is there room for improvement?

Tip: You cannot get perfect overnight. Six Sigma is a journey. Adopt Continuous Improvement mindset & culture

Sigma Level	Performance	DPMO	Yield
6	World Class	3.4	99.9997%
5		233	99.976%
4	Average	6,210	99.4%
3		66,807	93%
2	Non Competitive	308,537	65%
1		500,000	50%

Chapter 5 Lean Six Sigma

Lean Six Sigma DMAIC

Lean Six Sigma (LSS) blends Lean tools into Six Sigma's DMAIC framework:

Phases:

1. **Define** – Define the problem
2. **Measure** – Collect the Data
3. **Analyze** – Analyze the data, conduct Root-cause analysis
4. **Improve** – Identify a solution, verify it, implement
5. **Control** – Monitor performance, Sustain the solution

Let's unwrap each phase ...

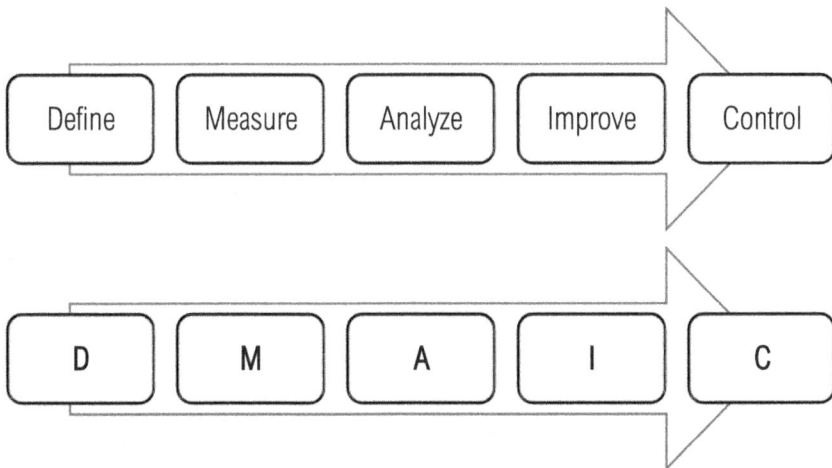

| Define | Measure | Analyze | Improve | Control |

| D | M | A | I | C |

Define Phase

DMAIC Phase 1 – Define

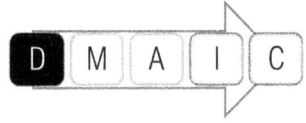

D M A I C

Define Phase is the first phase of Lean Six Sigma improvement process, includes:

- Outlining a Problem Statement
- Developing a Project Charter
- Establishing a Team
- Creating a SIPOC with High Level Current State Process Map

Tips:
- Keep your Charter & Process maps simple
- Focus on improvements in single functional area
- Aim for 30 to 90-day improvement project

Problem Statement

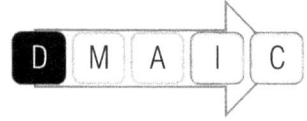

A good problem statement includes the following:

- Problem description in terms of metrics
- Process name and location
- Duration or time frame
- Size, magnitude or significance

Examples:

- In the last 12 months, 16% of our utility customers are late in paying their bills. This represents 22% of our outstanding receivables & negatively affects our operating cash flow at an average of $220,000 per month.
- In the 3rd quarter of 2019, about 27% of customers of West branch had to be re-billed, resulting in non-budgeted rebilling cost of $ 48,884, delayed accounts receivables by an average of 12.5 days, and increase in customer dissatisfaction.

Tips:
- Keep the audience in mind, convince management to provide resources & enlist team members
- Do not include speculations, probable causes, solutions

Project Charter Template

Organization		Service Line	
Project Name		Status	
Project Sponsor/s		Date	
Project Lead/s		Project Number	

Business Case	
Problem Statement	
Goal Statement	
Primary Measure	
High-level Timeline	
Project Scope	
Project Team	
Stakeholders	
Approvers	
Constraints	
Dependencies	
Risks	

Tip: Create this document. This formalizes the effort, team understanding, supports actions, sets time & target. Otherwise it's words in ether!

Business Case – Cost & Benefit Statement

Problem Statement – Clear, brief, quantifiable

Goal Statement – Summarize the goal of the project

Primary Measure – Measure in focus (Ex: Profit, Time or Quality)

High Level Timeline – Estimated timeline

Project Scope – What's in & out of scope. Start-End of a process

Project Team – Members, Subject Matter Experts, etc.

Stakeholders – Departments, functions, vendors, customers, etc. affected by the project

Approvers – Approval authority – Managers, Committee, Legal, Board, Council etc.

Constraints – Time, human resources, capital, policies, regulations etc.

Dependencies – List project dependencies or critical path items

Risks – List project risks, brand risks, financial, litigation risks

Establish a Team

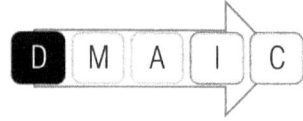

Key Members:

- Project Sponsor/s

- Project Lead or Co-leads

- Team members

- Appropriate Functional area representatives

- Optional: Subject Matter Experts, Consultants

Tips:

- Start small, if you need more members, you can add them later with your Sponsors support.

- Setup team meetings, agenda, minutes, issues, track progress, tasks, etc.

- Communicate & meet regularly

Measure Phase

DMAIC Phase 2 – Measure

D **M** A I C

Measure is the Second phase of Lean Six Sigma improvement process. Your focus here is to collect data based on your Define phase information such as, problem statement, SIPOC, etc. In this phase, you create a plan for data collection such as what to measure, determine the source of your data, collect the data & plot it. This will prepare you for the next phase of DMAIC – the Analyze phase.

For example: If your problem statement was, profits are trending down. Obtain data for Income & expenses for the last 12 months.

In this phase, key members of the team focus on:

- Collecting Data
- Measurement Plan
- Creating Trend, Histogram or Pareto Chart
- Creating Value Stream Map (if applicable)
- Validate or update Problem statement

Tips:
- Charts can be plotted in Excel or statistical software
- If data is not readily available, observations and time-study can be conducted

---

Measurement Plan

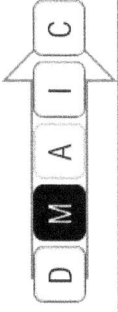

List the Metrics

- Outcome Measures – measures the outcomes produced by a process, also known as the lagging measure.
- Process Measures – measures process step/s, also known as leading measures, that tells if a process is in control
- Balanced Measures –measures to ensure the change will not impact other important measures negatively.

Metrics Definition

- Notate Process Start and End Points & notate the Formula (if any)
- Develop measurement plan (see Table)
- Obtain data or Measure

Tips:
- Start with a few key measures, you can always add more later, if necessary
- Look for historical data, if not, watch the process & obtain your new data

Metric Type	What is being measured?	Why is it being measured?	How is it measured (math)? What is the Source?	What is the target range?	What is the baseline data?	How is data collected, by whom, frequency?	Who collects or provides data and how?	Who reviews data and takes action?
Process Metric 1								
Process Metric 2								
Outcome Metric 1								
Outcome Metric 2								
Balanced Metric 1								
Balanced Metric 2								

Trend Chart Tool

Trend Charts are common these days, they show trends of data over time. Example: Stock market. Single point of measurement is misleading, hence measurements are taken at different times and frequency to obtain a better understanding - hourly, weekly, monthly, etc.

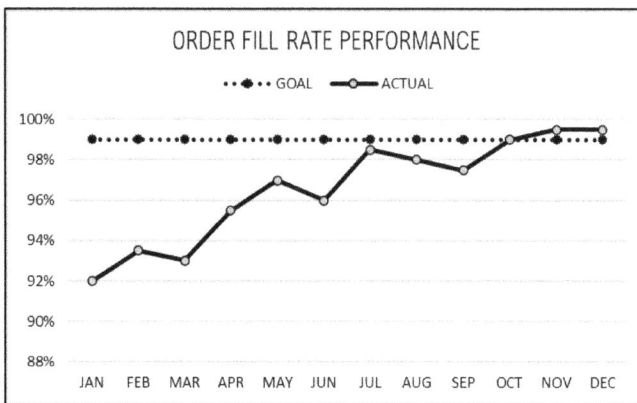

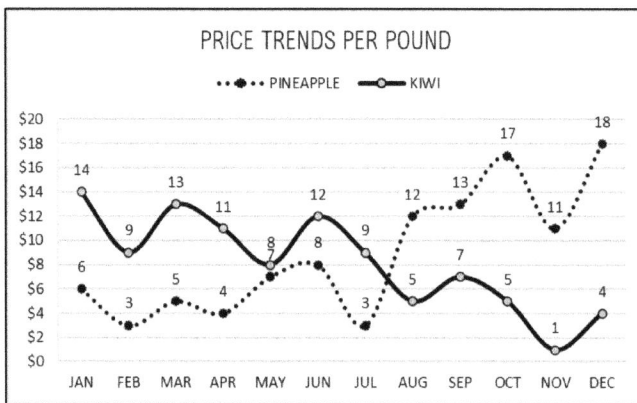

ORDER FILL RATE PERFORMANCE
•••◆••• GOAL —○— ACTUAL

PRICE TRENDS PER POUND
•••◆••• PINEAPPLE —○— KIWI

Tip: You can plot these using graph paper or use Microsoft Office Tools such as Excel — You can find tutorials on YouTube

Histogram Tool

Histograms show frequency of data in successive numerical intervals of equal size.

- Very important to understand the distribution or spread of the data for a process
- Normal distribution, is symmetric about the mean and appears as a bell curve.

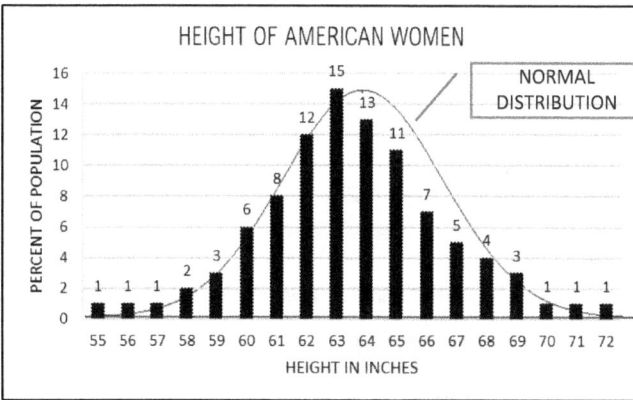

HEIGHT OF AMERICAN WOMEN

NORMAL DISTRIBUTION

PERCENT OF POPULATION

HEIGHT IN INCHES

Tip: You can plot these using graph paper or use Microsoft Office Tools such as Excel – You can find tutorials on YouTube

Pareto Chart Tool

Pareto principle states, 20% of factors cause 80% of effects. Also known as 80-20 rule. Pareto Chart, is a popular LSS Tool, shows percentage of effects caused by various contributors (reasons) such as frequency, time or cost. Focus efforts on largest contributors.

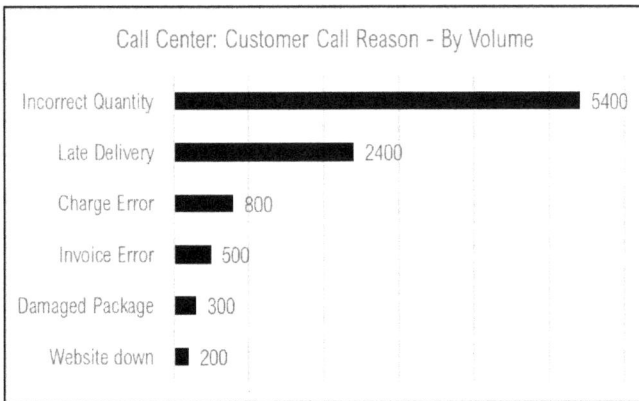

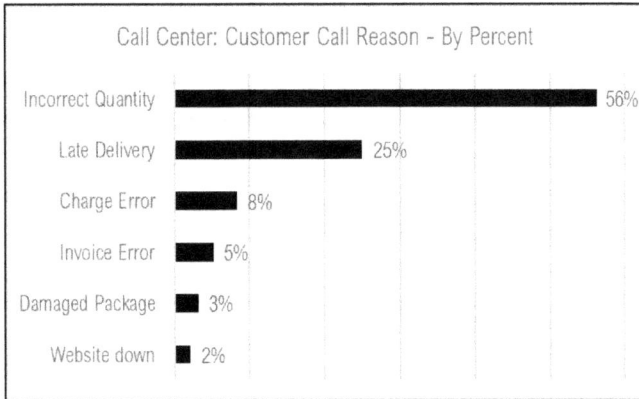

Call Center: Customer Call Reason - By Volume

Incorrect Quantity	5400
Late Delivery	2400
Charge Error	800
Invoice Error	500
Damaged Package	300
Website down	200

Call Center: Customer Call Reason - By Percent

Incorrect Quantity	56%
Late Delivery	25%
Charge Error	8%
Invoice Error	5%
Damaged Package	3%
Website down	2%

Tip: Pick the top 1 or 2 largest contributors (reasons) & find solutions. Once these are addressed, solve the next in line.

Value Stream Map

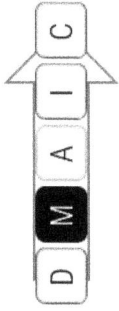

Optional: Value stream mapping allows you conduct Value Stream Analysis & spotlight opportunities for improvements.

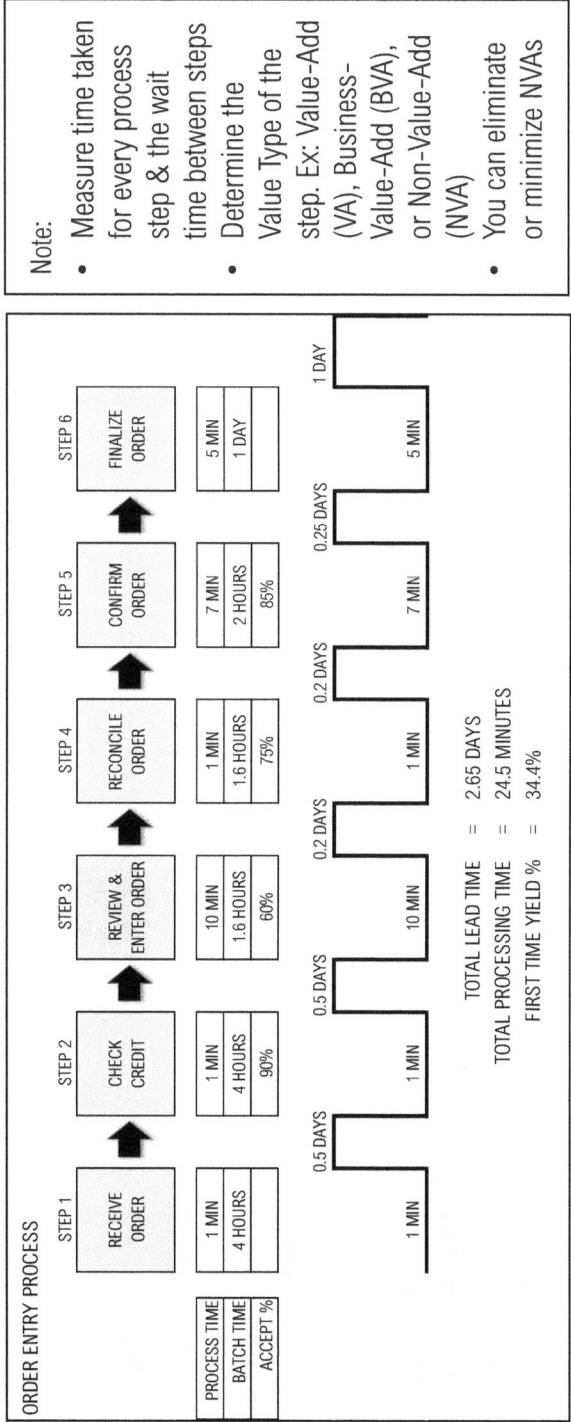

Note:
- Measure time taken for every process step & the wait time between steps
- Determine the Value Type of the step. Ex: Value-Add (VA), Business-Value-Add (BVA), or Non-Value-Add (NVA)
- You can eliminate or minimize NVAs

ORDER ENTRY PROCESS

	STEP 1 RECEIVE ORDER	STEP 2 CHECK CREDIT	STEP 3 REVIEW & ENTER ORDER	STEP 4 RECONCILE ORDER	STEP 5 CONFIRM ORDER	STEP 6 FINALIZE ORDER
PROCESS TIME	1 MIN	1 MIN	10 MIN	1 MIN	7 MIN	5 MIN
BATCH TIME	4 HOURS	4 HOURS	1.6 HOURS	1.6 HOURS	2 HOURS	1 DAY
ACCEPT %		90%	60%	75%	85%	

Wait times: 0.5 DAYS | 0.5 DAYS | 0.2 DAYS | 0.2 DAYS | 0.25 DAYS | 1 DAY

Processing times: 1 MIN | 1 MIN | 10 MIN | 1 MIN | 7 MIN | 5 MIN

TOTAL LEAD TIME	= 2.65 DAYS
TOTAL PROCESSING TIME	= 24.5 MINUTES
FIRST TIME YIELD %	= 34.4%

Analyze Phase

D M **A** I C

DMAIC Phase 3 – Analyze

Analyze Phase is the third phase of Lean Six Sigma improvement process. Your focus here is to now Analyze the data collected & inferences from the tools in Measure phase to find the source of your problem. Once determined, you are ready for the next DMAIC phase – Improve.

In this phase, key members of the team focus on:

- Pursuing Root-Cause Analysis (5-whys)
- Creating a Fishbone Diagram
- Analyzing Data – charts, trends of primary metric & factors
- Pursuing Root-cause verification

Tip: Data analysis can be done in Excel or statistical software – You can find tutorials on YouTube

Root-Cause Analysis (RCA)

Root-cause analysis is a method to identify the cause of a problem. It is important to understand the Cause and Effect relationship. Identifying the cause helps us in addressing the problem or situation with appropriate countermeasures or solutions in next phase.

Key tools to pursue root-cause analysis –

- Five Whys
- Cause & Effect or Fishbone Diagram

Note: Sometimes, analysis may determine need for collecting additional data. Revise your Measurement Plan accordingly.

Tip: A good team with diverse background & experience is very helpful.

RCA – 5 WHYS

5 Whys method

- Start by asking "Why" the effect happened

- Ask "Why" to the response given

- This gets you closer to the root-cause

- Usually asking Why 5 times gets you to the cause of the problem (sometimes more)

EXAMPLE: PROBLEM - WRONG ITEM SHIPPED TO CLIENT

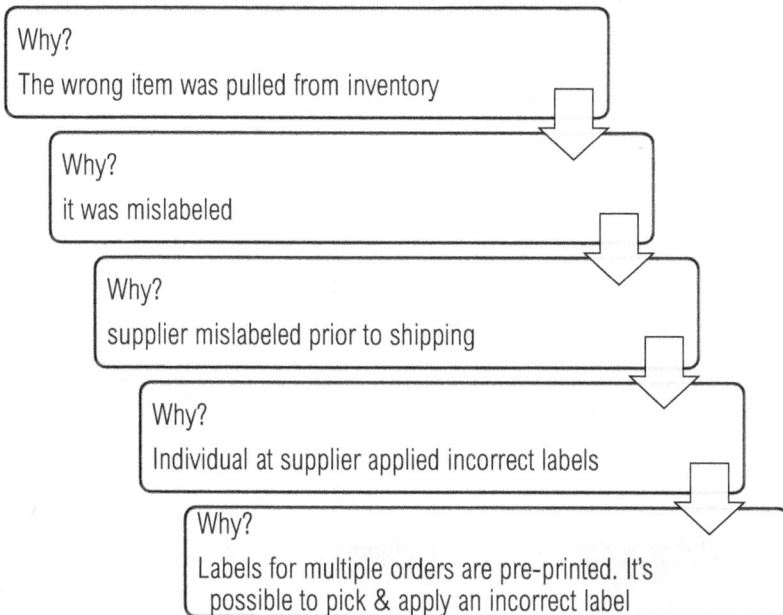

Why?
The wrong item was pulled from inventory

Why?
it was mislabeled

Why?
supplier mislabeled prior to shipping

Why?
Individual at supplier applied incorrect labels

Why?
Labels for multiple orders are pre-printed. It's possible to pick & apply an incorrect label

RCA – Cause & Effect Diagram

Also known as Fishbone Diagram, this diagram helps you to visually capture causes & sub-causes of a problem.

- Categories – typically categories include People, Process, Equipment, Material, Management, or Environment
- Causes – are deeper layers within the categories, known as Primary, Secondary, Tertiary, etc. causals

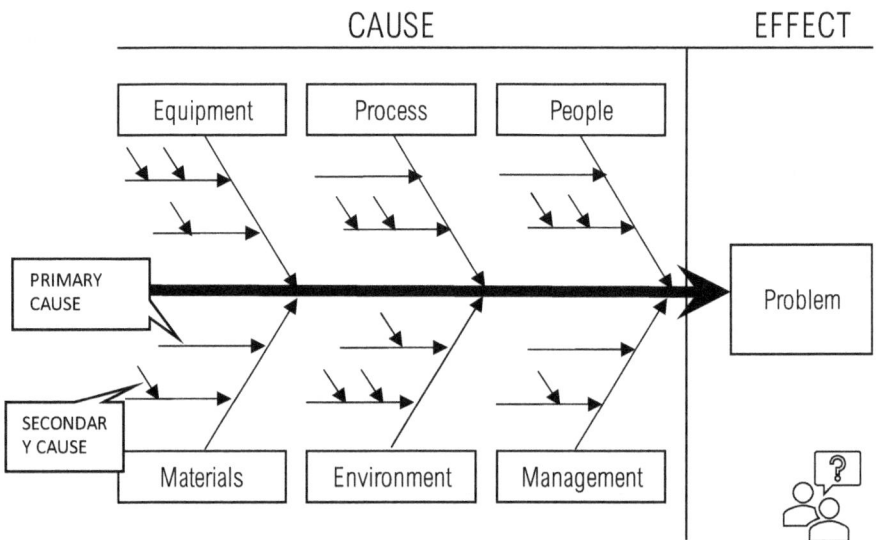

CAUSE   EFFECT

| Equipment | Process | People |

PRIMARY CAUSE

Problem

SECONDARY CAUSE

| Materials | Environment | Management |

Tip: You can use categories specific to your problem or situation

Cause & Effect – Illustration

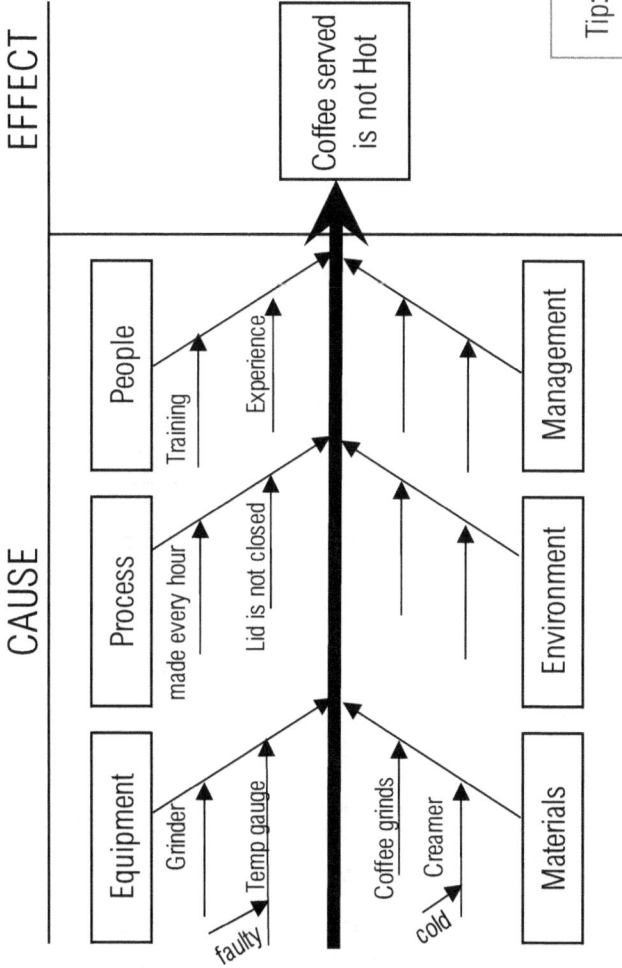

EFFECT

CAUSE

Coffee served is not Hot

People
- Training
- Experience

Process
- made every hour
- Lid is not closed

Equipment
- Grinder
- Temp gauge — faulty

Management

Environment

Materials
- Coffee grinds
- Creamer — cold

Tip:

Helps you seek out all
potential sources of causals

Data Analysis – Illustration

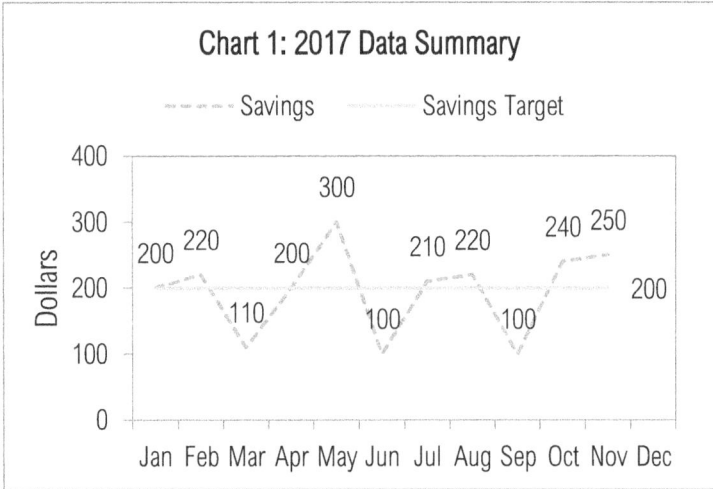

Chart 1: 2017 Data Summary

- - - - - Savings   Savings Target

Per Chart 1, it appears Savings is less in March, June, September. Let's find out how much we spent.

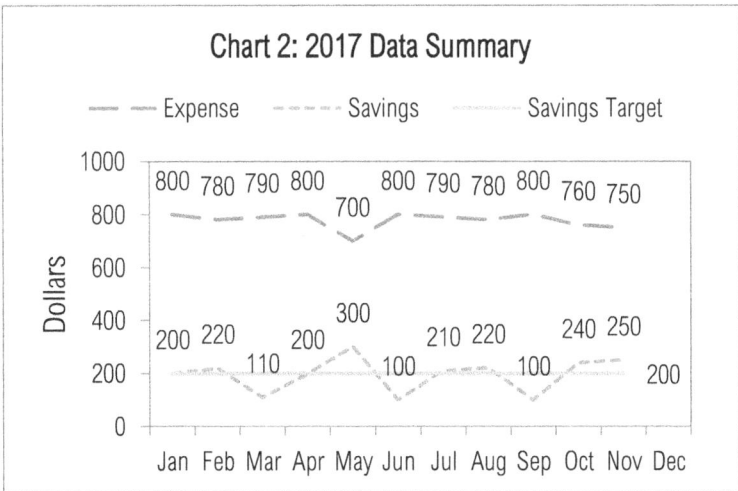

Chart 2: 2017 Data Summary

- - - Expense   - - - - Savings   Savings Target

Per Chart 2, Expense appears to be consistent, but does not explain lower savings in March, June, September. Let's check income

Data Analysis – Illustration

Chart 3: 2017 Data Summary

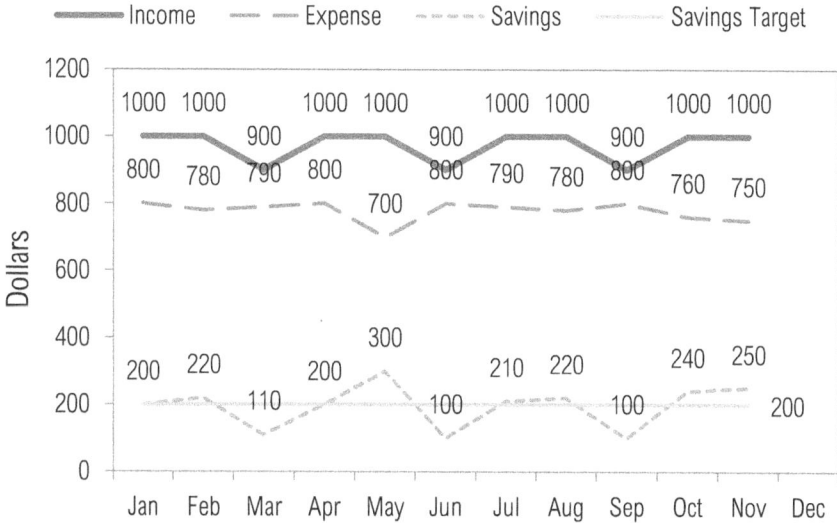

──── Income   ── ── Expense   – – – Savings   ········ Savings Target

Ah ha ! Now we can see the connection, the causal, every month the income lowers, the savings is lower. But why is this happening? Determine the root-cause for lower income during those months.

Improve Phase

DMAIC Phase 4 – Improve

Improve Phase is the fourth phase of Lean Six Sigma improvement process. Once team determines additional analysis is not necessary, and has identified the source or sources of the problem, it is time to find a solution.

In this phase, key members of the team:

- Listing potential improvement solutions. Evaluate pros and cons of every solution

- Developing Future State Process or Value Stream Map

- Piloting a solution for a limited time. Testing a solution before it is implemented in a Live environment

- Verifying if results align with problem statement (Tip: use Measurement plan used in measure phase)

- Implementing solution in Live environment

Tip: Conduct brainstorming sessions to list ideas. Sometimes a combination of multiple ideas may lead to a solution.

Identifying Solutions

- Brainstorming
    - Use team approach, gather all ideas
- Affinity Diagrams
    - Group all ideas by theme or affinities (see examples)
- Create Future State Process Maps
- Prioritizing and selecting solution
    - Use pair-wise or other solution selection methods
    - Ranking solutions can also be done based on availability of funds, resources, technology, etc.

Tip: Use white boards or easels to communicate ideas by writing or drawing. Beverages, candies or food are also helpful.

Process – Illustration

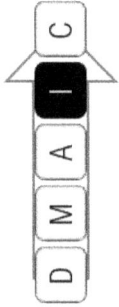

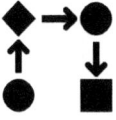

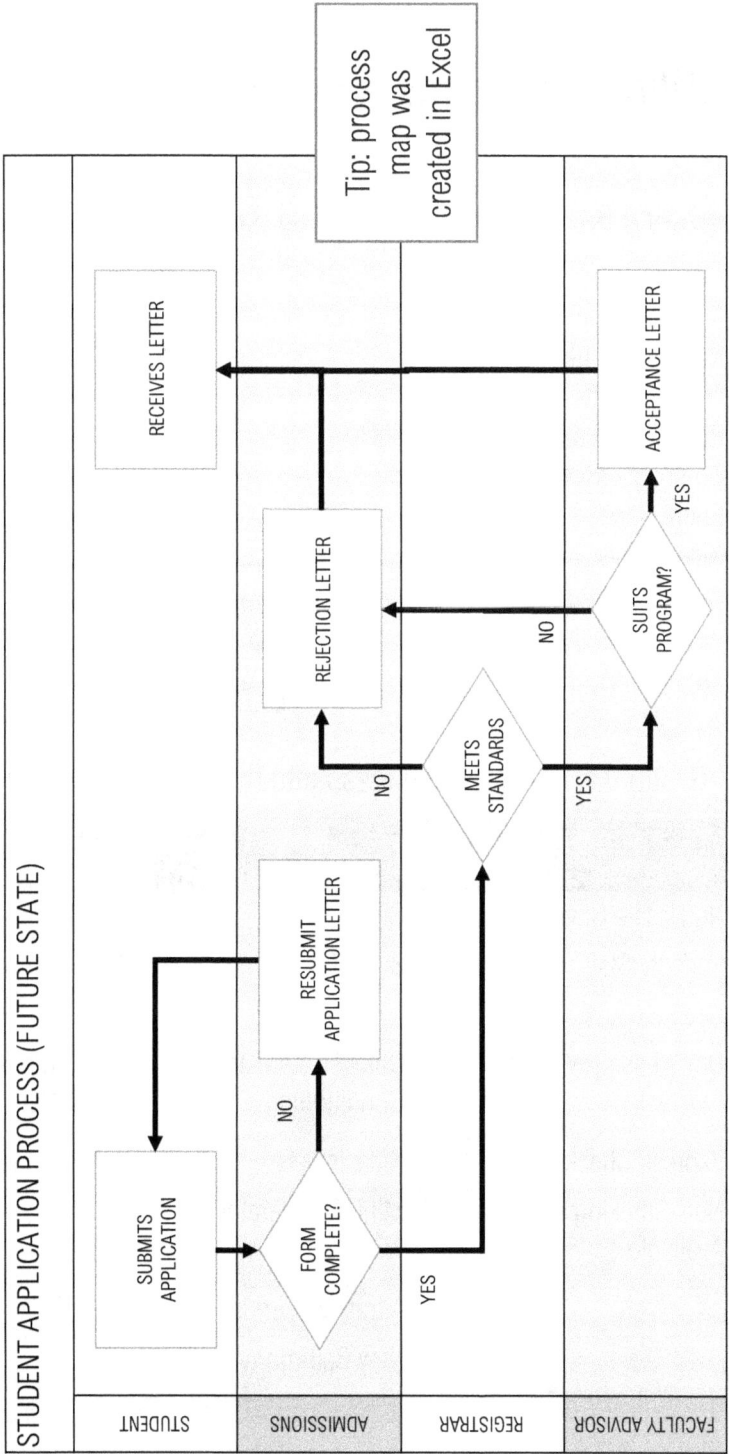

D M A I C

STUDENT APPLICATION PROCESS (FUTURE STATE)

Tip: process map was created in Excel

STUDENT
- SUBMITS APPLICATION
- RECEIVES LETTER

ADMISSIONS
- FORM COMPLETE?
  - NO → RESUBMIT APPLICATION LETTER
  - YES
- REJECTION LETTER

REGISTRAR
- MEETS STANDARDS
  - NO → REJECTION LETTER
  - YES

FACULTY ADVISOR
- SUITS PROGRAM?
  - NO
  - YES → ACCEPTANCE LETTER

Affinity Diagrams – Illustration

During Brainstorming jot down all the ideas

Clean Room	New Bathroom
Reliable Room Service	Good Room Service Selection
No Hassle Check In/Out	Mini-Refrigerator
Friendly Staff	Attractive Furnishings
Room Service Food Fresh & Hot	Big TV
Don't Lose Reservation	Express Checkout
Room Service Available	Quiet Heater/Air Conditioning
Nice Towels	Non-Smoking Room Available

Group the Brainstormed ideas into themes (as shown below)

Theme 1 - Check In/Out	Theme 2 - Room Quality	Theme 3 - Room Service
No Hassle Check In/Out	Clean Room	Room Service Available
Friendly Staff	Big TV	Good Room Service Selection
Don't Lose Reservation	Quiet Heater/Air Conditioning	Room Service Food Fresh & Hot
Express Checkout	Nice Towels	Reliable Room Service
Non-Smoking Room Available	Mini-Refrigerator	
	Attractive Furnishings	
	New Bathroom	

Decision-making – Illustration

Pair Wise Method for solution selection

One of the best ways to make a decision, when you are faced with multiple choices or solutions. You have to decide which one of these 4 options or solutions in front of you, A, B, C or D is the best.

- See table below, compare 2 options at a time, for instance compare A & B, if A is better, then write A in the appropriate box, then compare A & C, if A is better, then write A in the appropriate box, and so on.

- Add the totals in the Score Column, for Row A, A appears twice, write 2 in Score Column, repeat for B, C & D. Finally in the Rank column give the 1st or Top rank to the highest score and last rank to the lowest score.

	A	B	C	D	SCORE	RANK
A	-	A	A	D	2	2
B	A	-	C	D	0	4
C	A	C	-	D	1	3
D	D	D	D	-	3	1

Control Phase

DMAIC Phase 5 – Control

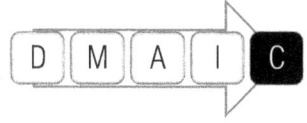

D M A I C

Control Phase is the final phase. Focus is on how to monitor & control an improvement in order to sustain it.

In this phase, key members of the team:

- Monitoring solution performance for a limited time (30-90 days) using the Control Plan
- If target is not being achieved, ensure solution is appropriately deployed, identify deviations and correct them
- Once target is being achieved consistently, reduce monitoring frequency

Tip: Conduct Brainstorming session.

Control Plan – Template

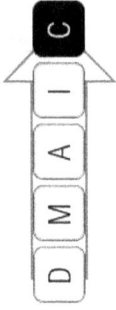

Include Outcome, Process & Balanced Measures

- Outcome Measures – measures the outcomes produced by a process, also known as the lagging measure.
- Process Measures – measures process metric, also known as leading measures, that tells if a process is in control
- Balanced Measures –measures to ensure the change will not impact other important measures negatively.

#	Type	Measure Name	Operational Definition	Target	Baseline Data	Data Source	Data Location	Frequency of data	Monitored by	Who takes action to correct performance	Response Plan including escalation	Sustainability Measures, Culture, etc.
1	Outcome											
2	Outcome											
3	Process											
4	Balanced											

Control Plan – Illustration

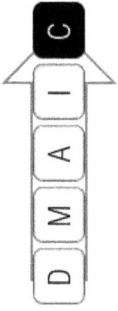

D M A **C** I

Pro Tip:

- This document is developed with Process Owner & Stakeholders
- This document ownership remains with Process Owner to ensure sustainability of performance

#	Type	Measure Name	Operational Definition	Target	Baseline Data	Data Source	Data Location	Frequency of data	Monitored by	Who takes action to correct performance	Response Plan including escalation	Sustainability Measures, Culture, etc.
1	Outcome	Order-to-Delivery	Cust Order to Cust receiving food	30 minutes	50 minutes in year 2020	Dashboard	Intranet Link	Bi-weekly	Director	Director	Address root-cause. Review with Department VP	Provide training to existing & new employees
2	Outcome	Preparation time	Cust Order to Meal ready	10 minutes	21 minutes in year 2020	ABC Report	ABC System	Weekly	Manager	Manager	Share with Director	Provide training to existing & new employees
3	Process											
4	Balanced											

Closing the project

All the good work is done, it is now time to:

- Hand-off all work products, project files, & Control plan to responsible functional leader
- Hold a Lessons learned session with Team members
- Save the project documents in archives for future reference
- Publish 1 or 2 page project info-graphic for awareness within the organization or at an industry forum
- Congratulate and recognize the team members
- Celebrate!

Chapter 6 Case Studies

Case Study 1: Reducing Patient Falls ... 1

Define Phase

Problem: In a surgical ward, patient falls were rising, creating safety risks and lengthening recovery times.

Goal: Reduce the fall rate by 50% within six months.

- Baseline Fall Rate: 5 falls per 1,000 patient days
- Target Fall Rate: 2.5 falls per 1,000 patient days

Measure Phase

The team collected data on falls over three months to identify patterns. Data included the time of day, patient age, location, and assistance levels.

Data Collected: Falls, Time, Location, Patient information. Findings:

- Fall Rate: 5 per 1,000 patient days
- Time of Day: Most falls occurred between 7 p.m. and 10 p.m.
- Location: Falls were concentrated near bathrooms and bedside areas.
- Patient Factors: High fall risk correlated with patients aged 70+.

Case Study 1: Reducing Patient Falls ... 2

Analyze Phase

The analysis identified key root causes:

- Low Staffing Levels at Night: Fewer nurses were available during evening hours, leading to delayed response times.
- Inadequate Patient Education: Many patients were unaware of the fall risks, especially after surgery.

Improve Phase

The team introduced several interventions:

- Medication reviews: Review a patient's medications for side effects and interactions that may increase the risk of falling
- Hourly Rounding for High-Risk Patients: Nurses checked in on high-risk patients hourly in the evening.
- Patient Education Program: Patients and families received fall prevention education upon admission.
- Non-slip footwear: Provide non-slip shoes or socks to help patients avoid slipping and tripping

Results

After implementing these interventions, the fall rate dropped significantly:

Metric	Pre-Improvement	Post-Improvement	% Change
Fall Rate (per 1,000 patient days)	5	2.3	-54%
Average Response Time	10 minutes	5 minutes	-50%

Control Phase

To sustain improvements, the unit implemented regular fall risk assessments and designated a fall prevention leader to monitor adherence to protocols, such as:

- Post-fall huddles: Hold post-fall team huddles to discuss falls.

- Auditing: Audit fall prevention practices.

- Monthly falls reporting: Track & Report falls monthly.

Case Study 2: Reducing Medication Errors ... 1

Define Phase

Problem: The pediatric unit faced medication delays and occasional dose errors, particularly during shift changes, impacting patient safety.

Goal: Reduce medication errors by 40% within three months.

- Baseline Error Rate: 7 errors per 1,000 doses
- Target Error Rate: 4 errors per 1,000 doses

Measure Phase

Data on medication errors was collected over two months, tracking error types, times, and staff involved.

Data Collected: Error rate, Time, & Types. Findings:

- Error Rate: 7 per 1,000 doses
- Time of Occurrence: Most errors occurred during shift handovers.
- Error Types: Predominantly dose miscalculations and timing delays.

Analyze Phase

The analysis identified key root causes:

- Handwritten Handover Notes: Medication notes during shift changes were sometimes illegible or incomplete.

- Lack of Clear Handover Protocols: Shift handovers lacked a standard process for medication information transfer.

Improve Phase

To reduce medication errors the team implemented:

- Electronic Medication Records: Nurses started using digital records, eliminating handwriting issues.

- Standardized SBAR Handover: The unit adopted SBAR for structured, medication-focused handovers.

- Double-check dosing, especially for high-alert medications. High-alert medications have a higher risk of causing harm if used incorrectly

- Update nurses' knowledge, especially about new medications

- Coaching to Nurses to ask for assistance when dealing with high volume or medically complex patients.

Case Study 2: Reducing Medication Errors ... 3

Results

Post-intervention, medication errors decreased substantially:

Metric	Pre-Improvement	Post-Improvement	% Change
Medication Error Rate (per 1,000 doses)	7	3.5	-50%

Control Phase

To sustain improvements, the unit implemented assessments & monitored adherence to protocols, such as:

- Quarterly training sessions were established to ensure adherence to SBAR handover protocols.

- Auditing: Regular Audit of error prevention practices.

- Huddles: Hold post-error team huddles to discuss errors.

- Monthly Medication error reporting: Track & Report errors monthly.

Patterns galore...

I am sure you are seeing a pattern to this 5-step DMAIC method & also realizing how practical it is for a team to make evidence-based improvements & sustain results.

Let's review a few more.

Case Study 3: Reducing Discharge Time... 1

Define Phase

Problem: Delayed discharges led to increased length of stay, bed shortages and patient frustration, with discharge times averaging four hours.

Goal: Reduce discharge times by 30% within three months.

- Baseline Discharge Time: 240 minutes (4 hours)
- Target Discharge Time: 168 minutes (2.8 hours)

Measure Phase

The team measured discharge times over a month, tracking the time taken for discharge summaries, medication orders, and final nurse checks.

Data Collected: Total Time taken for Discharge summaries, Medication orders, and Final nurse checks. Findings:

- Average Discharge Time: 240 minutes

Analyze Phase

The analysis highlighted a few key root causes:

- Delayed Discharge Summaries: Doctors often completed summaries in the afternoon, delaying the process.

- Medication Delays: Pharmacy requests were often submitted late, adding to discharge times.

Improve Phase

To speed up discharges, the team introduced:

- Morning Discharge Huddle: Nurses, Pharmacists and doctors identified likely discharges early, prioritizing these patients' paperwork and medications.

- Huddle protocol & report out script was established to enable quick report outs to keep the huddles short and effective.

- Standardized Discharge Checklist: Nurses used a checklist to streamline final patient checks and paperwork.

Case Study 3: Reducing Discharge Time ... 3

Results

The discharge time decreased significantly:

Metric	Pre-Improvement (minutes)	Post-Improvement (minutes)	% Change
Average Discharge Time	240	145	-40%

The final results of 145 minutes were better than pursued target of 168 minutes.

Control Phase

To sustain these results, the morning discharge huddle became a routine part of the workflow, and discharge times were monitored monthly to ensure sustained improvement.

During onboarding of new doctors, nurses, and pharmacists were provided orientation to huddle protocols & scripts.

Define Phase

Problem: Long wait times in the emergency department (ED) frustrated patients and staff. Nurses noticed that many patients were waiting over two hours to be seen, which affected patient satisfaction and created a bottleneck in the ED.

Goal: Reduce average patient wait time in the ED by 40% over six months.

- Current Average Wait Time: 120 minutes
- Target Wait Time: 30 minutes
- Scope: Focus on triage & initial assessment process.

Measure Phase

Nurses gathered data on wait times for three months, tracking each patient's time from arrival to triage and from triage to seen by a doctor.

Data Collected: Wait times, patient acuity level, staffing levels, & arrival times. Findings:

- Average Triage Wait: 45 minutes
- Average Wait for Doctor: 75 minutes
- Peak Hours observed: 10 a.m. to 4 p.m.

Case Study 4: Reducing Wait Times in ED ... 2

Analyze Phase

The team analyzed data to discover two root causes:

- High Variability in Triage Time: Triage times varied widely due to inconsistent staffing and a lack of streamlined protocols.

- Bottleneck at Doctor Assessment: Physicians were overwhelmed during peak hours, causing backlogs in initial patient evaluations.

Improve Phase

To address these causes, the team identified & developed three solutions:

- Rapid Triage Protocol: A triage nurse rapidly assesses each patient for 60–90 seconds to prioritize care

- Patient categorization: Patients are categorized as having emergency signs, priority signs, or no emergency or priority signs. Patients with emergency signs need immediate treatment, while those with priority signs are treated without delay. Non-urgent patients can wait their turn

- Physician Assistants for Peak Hours: Additional physician assistants were scheduled during peak hours to alleviate the load on doctors.

AIM - Lean Six Sigma in 60 minutes for
Nurses & Leaders

87

Results

After implementing these changes, the team measured wait times:

Metric	Pre-Improvement (minutes)	Post-Improvement (minutes)	% Change
Average Triage Wait	45	9	-80%
Average Wait for Doctor	75	19	-75%
Total Wait Time	120	28	-77%

The final results of 28 minutes were within the target of 30 minutes.

Patient Satisfaction results improved as well.

Control Phase

To sustain these results,

- The ED implemented regular monitoring of wait times.

- Adjusted staffing schedules every quarter based on peak time data.

- Nurses received refresher training quarterly on the rapid triage protocol to ensure consistency.

Case Study 5: Reducing CLABSI in ICU ... 1

Define Phase

Problem: The ICU team observed a high rate of central line-associated bloodstream infections (CLABSIs), impacting patient recovery times and increasing hospital costs.

Goal: Reduce the CLABSI rate by 60% in the ICU within one year.

- Current CLABSI Rate: 5.2 infections per 1,000 central line days
- Target Rate: 2.0 infections per 1,000 central line days

Measure Phase

Data was gathered over six months, tracking the incidence of CLABSIs, patient demographics, line insertion methods, and maintenance practices.

Data Collected: Infection rates, compliance with sterile techniques, and frequency of line care practices. Findings:

- Compliance with Sterile Technique: 72%
- Infection Rate: 5.2 infections per 1,000 line days

Analyze Phase

The team used fishbone diagrams and root cause analysis to uncover the following contributing factors:

- Inconsistent Use of Sterile Techniques: Nurses and physicians sometimes deviated from protocols.

- Poor Line Maintenance Documentation: Inconsistent documentation made it difficult to ensure proper care routines.

Improve Phase

To address these issues, the ICU implemented two key changes:

- Strict Sterile Technique Protocol: All staff received refresher training on sterile techniques, and checklists were introduced to ensure compliance.

- Daily Line Review: A dedicated "line champion" nurse checked each central line daily to ensure protocol adherence and proper maintenance.

Results

After six months, the ICU tracked a significant decrease in CLABSI rates:

Metric	Pre-Improvement	Post-Improvement	% Change
Compliance with Sterile Technique	72%	95%	+23%
CLABSI Rate (per 1,000 days)	5.2	2.1	-60%

Control Phase

To sustain these improvements,

- The ICU maintained monthly audits on sterile technique compliance
- Continued the daily line review with the line champion role.
- Additionally, CLABSI rates were reported in monthly staff meetings to encourage continued focus.

Life made easier

Imagine you used this 5-step DMAIC method & in a few months you solved a couple of notable problems.

_____

How would this impact the people you care?

♥

How would this impact your life?

♥

How would you feel?

♥

_____

Jot down your improvement ideas & get started now !

Bonus Content
3 Things For Nurses To Reduce Stress

Mindfulness and Breathing Exercises

- Tool: Apps like Headspace or Calm offer quick mindfulness exercises, meditation, & breathing techniques that nurses can do on breaks.
- Benefit: Helps center focus, manage stress, and improve resilience, even during high-pressure shifts.

Time Management Techniques

- Tool: Pomodoro Technique or Time Blocking allows nurses to break their day into focused segments with planned breaks.
- Benefit: Enhances productivity, ensures time for breaks, and prevents burnout from constant multitasking.

Physical Wellness Strategies

- Tool: You are worth it, take 3 minutes for yourself to stretch, relax your shoulders, hips, ankles, look outside the window to look at the sky, distant trees, people, any landscape or skyscape.
- Benefit: Short stretches or light exercises can improve physical well-being, release tension, and boost energy, which rejuvenates you throughout the day. In the long run, your eyes & body will thank you.

Congratulations

You made it!

You are now ready to apply these learnings & understandings!

Let's take this out for a spin.

Pick a small problem you want to solve.

Use the *LSS DMAIC Checklist* on the next page.

Notes

LSS – DMAIC Checklist

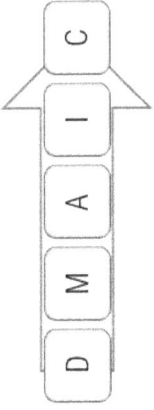

D M A I C

Tip: Use this single page view of all phases to track your progress during learning or projects

Define	Measure	Analyze	Improve	Control
☐ Outline a Problem Statement	☐ List Metrics & Definitions	☐ Analyze Data	☐ List solutions	☐ Monitor solution performance
☐ Develop a Project Charter	☐ Collect Data	☐ Pursue Root-Cause Analysis	☐ Develop Future State Process	☐ Achieve target
☐ Establish a Team	☐ Create Charts	☐ Create a Fishbone Diagram	☐ Pilot a solution	☐ Identify deviations & correct
☐ Create a SIPOC	☐ Create Value Stream Map (if applicable)	☐ Pursue Root-cause verification	☐ Verify results	
			☐ Implement solution